CLIL Readers

The world of plants

written by
Jimmy Singh

Richmond

Plants are very important. They provide animals with oxygen and food.
Plants are living things. They always stay in the same place. They cannot move about.

We do not know exactly how many different plants there are in the world, but we do know there are over three hundred thousand types of plants.

Most plants have three different parts. The roots, the stem and the leaves. Each part is very important for the survival of the plant.

The roots fix the plant to the ground. They also absorb water and minerals. Most roots grow deep into the ground, but some can grow above ground like mangroves.

The stem is the part that supports the plant. The stem of a tree is called a trunk. The tallest tree is a redwood and it is one hundred and fifteen metres tall!

Leaves absorb carbon dioxide from the air. This helps the plant to make its own food using a process called photosynthesis.

Some plants lose their leaves in autumn and winter. These are called deciduous. Evergreen plants keep their leaves all year round.

Many plants have flowers. Flowers can be many different colours, shapes and sizes. The biggest flower in the world is the *Rafflesia arnoldii*. It can be more than one metre in diameter.

Insects are very important for plants. Bees use the nectar from flowers to make honey. When they collect the nectar, they carry pollen from one flower to another. This is how reproduction begins.

Some animals use plants to make their homes. Many birds build nests on tree branches. They are made from leaves, grass and small twigs.

Some animals eat plants. For example, panda bears eat a lot of bamboo. They can spend twelve hours eating every day!

Some plants can capture animals. The Venus flytrap captures insects and spiders. If insects touch the inside of the plant, it closes its trap immediately.

Some plants produce food like fruit, vegetables and grains. These have vitamins and fibre which help people stay healthy.

People also use many different plants as medicine. For example, an infusion of camomile flowers helps cure stomach ache.

Plants can also be dangerous. The oleander is a beautiful plant, but if you eat it, you can get a terrible stomach ache. You must never eat plants or flowers that you do not know.